THE BEST BOOK OF

Trains

Richard Balkwill

KINGFISHER

BOSTON

Contents

4 The first railroads

6 A faster way to travel

Author: Richard Balkwill
Senior editor: Sarah Milan
Design director: Mike Davis
Production controller: Kelly Johnson
Illustrators: Tom Connell, Chris
Forsey, Peter Bull, Mike Atkinson,
Richard Draper

Drawings page 12 top right and page
13 top left © Venice Simplon-Orient-
Express Limited

KINGFISHER
a Houghton Mifflin Company imprint
222 Berkeley Street
Boston, Massachusetts 02116
www.houghtonmifflinbooks.com

First published in 1999
10 9 8 7 6 5

5TR/1103/WKT/MA(MA)/128KMA
Copyright © Kingfisher Publications Plc 1999

LIBRARY OF CONGRESS CATALOGING-IN-PUBLICATION DATA
Balkwill, Richard.
   The best book of trains/by Richard Balkwill.—1st ed.
    p.cm.
   Summary: Introduces all sorts of trains from around
the world, covering different types of trains, how they
are constructed and how they run, who drives them,
and more.
   1. Railroads—Trains—Juvenile literature.
[1. Railroads—Trains.]
TF148.B24   1999
625.'1—dc21 99-12757 CIP

ISBN 0-7534-5200-6
Printed in Hong Kong

14 Powered by diesel

16 Pulling a load

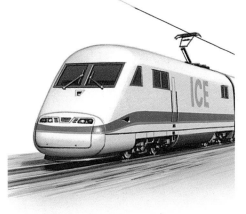

24 Tunnels and bridges

26 High-speed trains

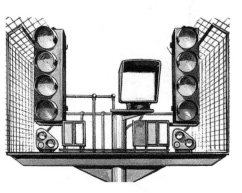

The first railroads

Over 250 years ago, railroads in Europe were being built to carry material from

mines. At first, these rails were made of flat stones laid in the ground. Loaded wagons could then run down a hill by force of gravity. Workers had to steer them to keep them from running off the rails. Soon, metal rails were laid down and flanges, or lips, on either side of the wheels kept the wagons on the rails. The distance between the rails was known as the gauge. By the early 1800s, inventors had found a way to power engines using steam from water heated by coal fires.

Horse power
Before the invention of steam engines, horses were often used to pull wagons along rails.

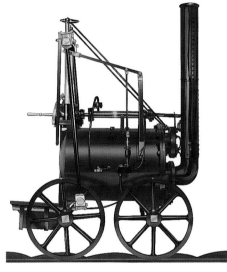

The first passenger railroad
By 1830, the English cities of Liverpool and Manchester were connected by rail. The 30-mile line was the first double-tracked railroad with passenger trains running on a regular schedule. The trip took about two hours.

Catch me who can
This was built in 1808 by Richard Trevithick, engineer of the world's first working steam locomotive in 1804.

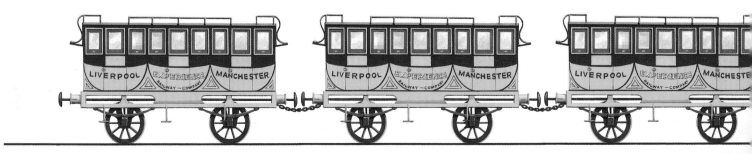

Stephenson's Rocket

This was designed and built in 1829 for trials on the Liverpool and Manchester Railway by George Stephenson and his son Robert. It reached a speed of 25 miles per hour.

Chimney and blowpipe

Multi-tubular boiler

Stoker

Engineer

Coal fire

Piston

Water barrel

Tender

Driving rod

Driving wheel

Flanged wheels

Wheels were made with a flange on either side to keep them from slipping off the rails.

Wheels without flanges

Wheels with flanges

A faster way to travel

In the 1850s, train travel completely changed the way people moved around the country. Before that, coaches drawn by teams of horses often took four days to travel 150 miles. In winter, the rough roads might be flooded or blocked by fallen trees. The new trains carried people the same distance in about four hours.

Paddington Station

This station, in London, England, was designed by English engineer Isambard Kingdom Brunel, and opened in 1854. From here, passengers could travel the 195 miles to Exeter on the Great Western Railroad.

The roof at Paddington Station was made up of great arches

Open-top cars

In the 1840s, rich people traveled in their own covered cars. The poor had to stand in open cars in the wind and rain, and smothered in smoke from the engine. By 1850, railroads provided cars for second and third class travelers with hard benches and a roof.

Porters secured baggage to the top of the train

In 1869, the two lines met at Promontory, Utah where the last spike was driven in

CALIFORNIA

Rocky Mountains

Green River

Sacramento

NEVADA

UTAH

Salt Lake City

Crossing the continent

The first railroad to cross an entire continent was built in the United States. It was completed in 1869, linking the country from coast to coast. The new railroad system allowed settlers to move all across the country in search of new land. But the track ran through territory that belonged to Native Americans, who called the train the "iron horse." They often attacked the railroad builders in defense of their land.

Steam power

This steam engine was typical of the kind used on the new railroad. It weighed about 40 tons and could travel at up to 19 miles per hour.

W.E.A.R.R.

A cowcatcher pushed cattl off the tracks

The Native Americans fought to protect their homeland

WYOMING

COLORADO

Cheyenne

North Platte

KANSAS

Omaha

Previously built railroad lines connected the new line to the East Coast

Meeting in the middle

The Central Pacific started laying track eastward from Sacramento, while the Union Pacific laid track westward from Omaha. When finished in 1869, the line ran for 1,078 miles.

Bridges of iron and wood were built to cross valleys

Many of the workers were immigrants

Heavy work

Teams of workers laid track by fixing iron rails to wooden sleepers with spikes. In 1869, a record 10 miles of track was laid in one day by a team of 800 men.

Steam engines

Until the 1950s, most passenger and freight trains were hauled by steam locomotives. Coal (and sometimes oil) was burned to heat water and make steam at high pressure. This moved a piston back and forth, which drove the wheels. The advantage of these engines was the simplicity of their design. But they generated a lot of steam and smoke and had to carry their own supply of fuel on board. With the arrival of diesel and electric engines, the great age of steam came to an end.

Puffing uphill
In the Rocky Mountains of Colorado, old steam engines are still used to haul tourist trains on the Durango to Silverton line.

Steam in China
In China, where there is plenty of coal, steam locomotives were being built until 1995. Engines like this one are still widely used to haul both freight and passenger trains.

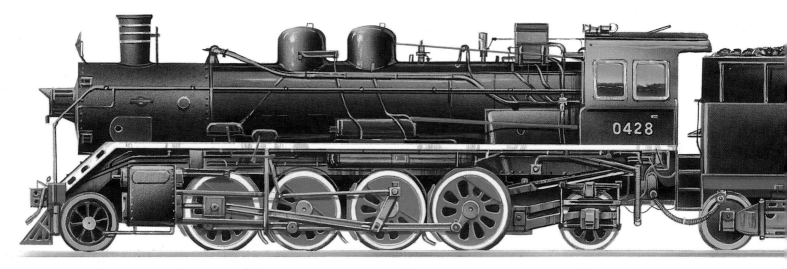

0428

Big Boy

The world's largest and most powerful steam engine is the 500-ton Big Boy. Twenty-five of these were built in the 1940s to haul freight trains in Utah.

Mallard

The world's fastest steam engine is the Mallard. In July 1938, this streamlined locomotive reached a speed of 125 miles per hour between Grantham and Peterborough in England.

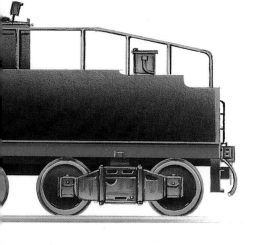

Traveling in luxury

During the 1850s, railroad companies began to build more comfortable passenger cars, especially in the U.S.A. and Europe. Many long-distance trains were now equipped with heating and lighting. In 1865, U.S. businessman George Pullman built the first sleeping car, which also had a bathroom. His name has been used to describe luxury cars for dining and sleeping ever since. This form of travel became very popular for those who could afford it. Today, many of the cars have been restored for use by tourists.

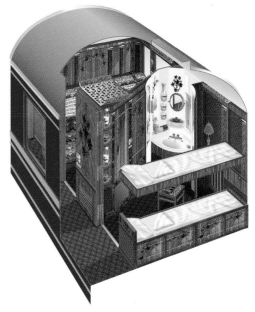

By night
Bunkbeds fold down from the walls. This compartment on the Venice Simplon-Orient-Express also contains a sink and hanging space for clothes.

Waiters serve meals to the passengers

VOITURE PULLM

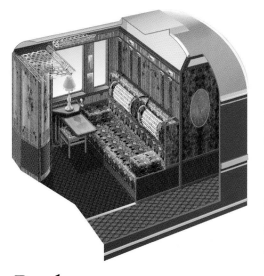

By day
The beds in the sleeping compartment fold away, leaving a comfortable sitting area.

Staff on board
The passengers on board the luxury trains are taken care of by staff trained as chefs, waiters, stewards, conductors, and porters.

Decorative panels line the walls

EUROPEENS

RROZZA – RISTORANTE

Traveling restaurant
The Lalique dining car, built in 1929 as a first-class Pullman, is one of the cars used on the Venice Simplon-Orient-Express, which runs on routes in Europe. The car is named after René Lalique, who designed its decorative panels.

Powered by diesel

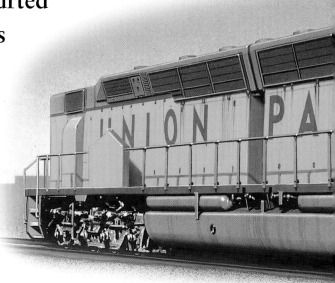

In the 1930s, diesel trains started running in countries such as the U.S.A. and Germany, where diesel was cheaper than coal. Most diesel engines power a generator that makes electricity. This drives a motor that turns the wheels. Like steam engines, diesel locomotives gave off fumes, but were easier to clean and maintain. Some were also very fast. The American Burlington Zephyr ran at an average speed of 83 miles per hour. By the late 1950s, most passenger trains in North America were hauled by diesels. Ten years later, steam engines had disappeared from almost all railroads in Europe and North America.

Longest and heaviest
The record-breaking Union Pacific Centennial diesel locomotive is nearly 100 feet long and weighs 229 tons.

Flying Hamburger
The German Fliegende (Flying) Hamburger trains ran between Hamburg and Berlin from 1932. They covered the 178 miles in under three hours at speeds of up to 100 miles per hour.

Double the power

Two diesel locomotives, one at each end,
power this nine-car, high-speed train
that travels at 125 miles per
hour between Aberdeen
and London in
Great Britain.

Pulling a load

Freight trains are often used for hauling goods over long distances. Loads of coal, oil, and raw materials such as steel and timber all go by rail. In large countries such as the U.S.A., Canada, and Australia, trains carry more freight than passengers. Although not as fast as planes or as convenient as trucks, trains can carry huge loads. A 100-car freight train might be 1.25 miles long. To move the same load by road, you would need 100 trucks and drivers.

Bulk carriers

Different types of carriers are used to transport different goods. Large tankers like this one are used to carry diesel and liquid gas.

Covering vast distances

Bulky freight such as coal, oil, and minerals is carried in specially designed wagons. These are often open-topped so that the wagons can be loaded on the move. Each wagon is fitted with its own set of air brakes, operated by the engineer.

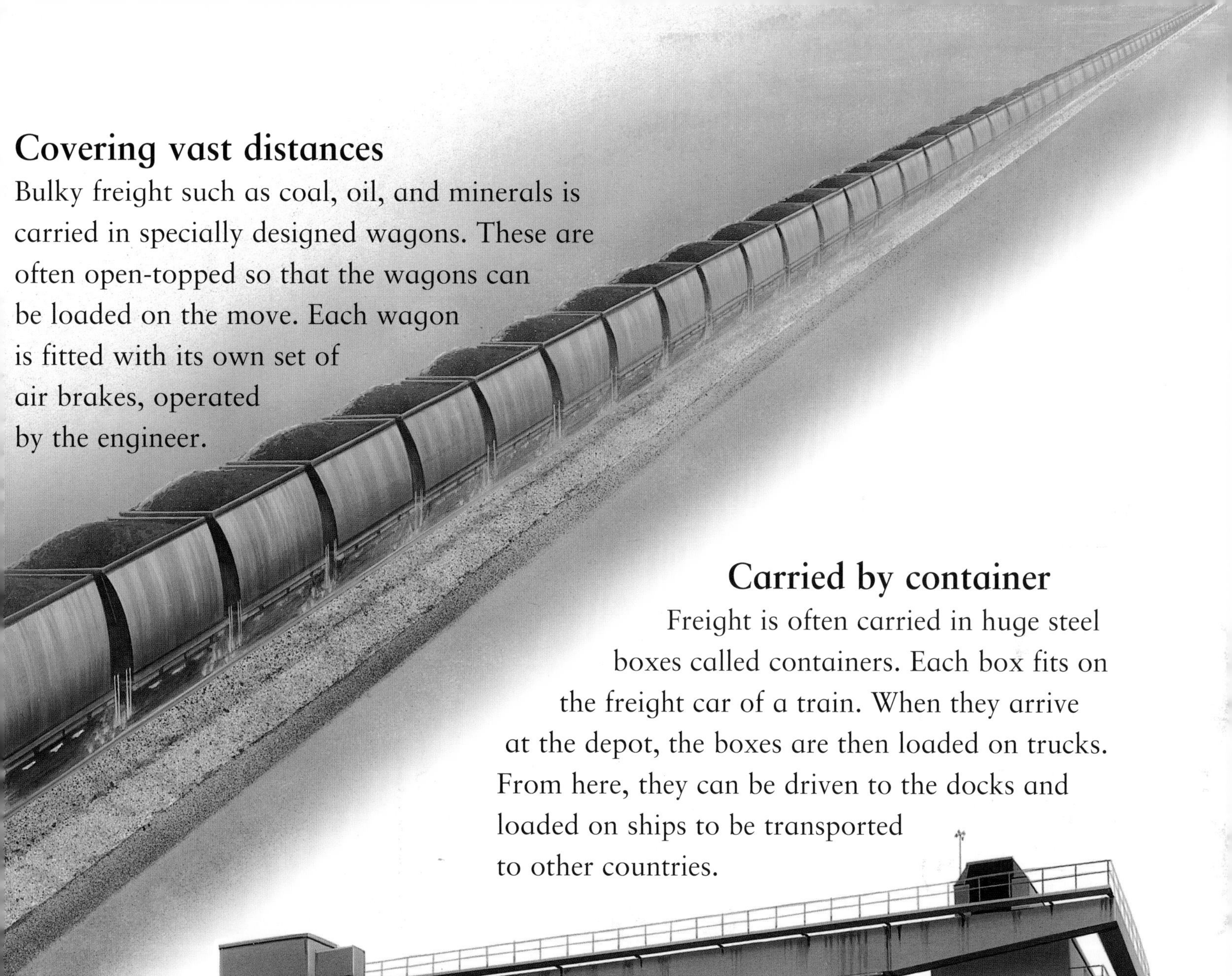

Carried by container

Freight is often carried in huge steel boxes called containers. Each box fits on the freight car of a train. When they arrive at the depot, the boxes are then loaded on trucks. From here, they can be driven to the docks and loaded on ships to be transported to other countries.

Container

Cranes lift the containers off the train and load them on trucks.

Freight car

Electric trains

During World War II (1939-45), many railroads were damaged. Whole sections of track in countries such as France and Germany were destroyed by bombs. After the war, they began to rebuild and electrify the old lines, as well as building new ones. Putting up the posts and wires that carry the power supply is expensive, but the trains run faster and do not produce smoke. Some countries, like Switzerland, have electrified most of their lines.

The electric current was taken in from the power line by a sliding frame called a pantograph

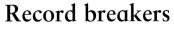

Early days of electricity
Built in 1895, this electric engine pulled trains through a 1.25-mile tunnel in Baltimore, Maryland. It replaced steam engines, which were filling the tunnel with smoke.

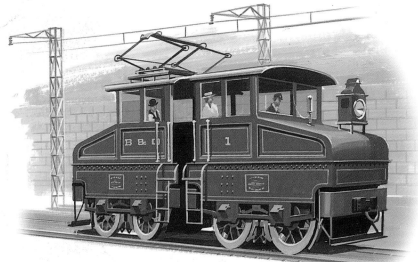

Record breakers
In 1955, near Bordeaux in France, two electric locomotives (CC-7107 and BB-9004), each hauling three coaches, reached a record speed of 207 miles per hour on two different days.

Glossary

bullet train A Japanese high-speed, streamlined train.

car An enclosed compartment on a train for carrying passengers. A car is also known as a coach.

diesel A fuel used to power diesel engines.

engine (1) Any machine that converts energy into mechanical work. (2) A railroad locomotive.

engineer (1) The driver of a train. (2) Someone who builds railroads or locomotives.

flange A lip on the metal wheel of a train that keeps it on the tracks and guides it around corners.

freight Goods transported in large quantities, often by rail.

gauge The width between the two rails on a railroad track. In North America and most of Europe, the gauge is 4 feet 8½ inches.

generator A machine that makes power or heat.

grade crossing The point at which a railroad and a road cross. It usually has barriers to close off the road when a train passes.

immigrant A person who has recently moved from one country to another.

locomotive An engine powered by steam, electricity, or diesel, used for pulling trains along railroad tracks.

maglev train A high-speed train that runs on magnets located in the train and on the track.

monorail A train that runs on a single rail.

points Rails in the track that move to guide the train onto a different route.

porter A person who carries passengers' baggage in a train station.

Pullman car A luxury car, where passengers can have meals and refreshments at every seat, or rest in a sleeping cabin.

rack railroad A steep railroad that uses a central rail linked to a cog wheel to guide the train up and down the track.

repel If two magnets repel each other, they push away from each other.

siding A short stretch of track connected to the main line where trains can wait.

signals Colored lights used to tell the engineer that the way ahead is clear.

sleeper A wooden block used to support the rails of a track.

span The distance between the two ends of a bridge.

steward A person on a train whose job is to help the passengers.

third rail A length of rail built beside the tracks that transmits electric power to the engine.

track A pair of parallel rails on which trains run.

wagon An open car used for carrying freight.

Index